Powers of Attorney:
Healthcare
Property

Pauline G. Dembicki
Attorney at Law

THIRD Edition

Cover art by Gadsavage

ISBN 13: 978-0692711460 (Pauline G. Dembicki)

ISBN 10: 0692711465

This book is intended as information about our legal system and is not intended as legal advice. Please talk to your attorney before writing your powers of attorney.

Laws vary among states and countries.

Powers of Attorney

Pauline G. Dembicki

Attorney at Law

Table of Contents

Author Forward

After practicing law for over thirty years, I see my work falling into two categories: planning and crisis management.

Planning is less expensive, has more options and less aggravation. It's a great way to protect your assets, decisions and loved ones. It gives you a chance to mull over your choices and finetune things to suit your needs.

To demystify and encourage estate planning, I lecture to community groups, explaining the options in estate planning, e.g. wills, trusts, and powers of attorney. At each lecture I caution the audience that my words of wisdom are not legal advice but general information about our legal system.

This book is not legal advice. It is general information about our legal system for you to consider before you meet with your lawyer.

Legal advice happens when you meet with a lawyer individually and agree to work together. There is usually a written agreement that describes the work contemplated, the costs, time frame and when payment is due.

The main chapters of this book focus on health care and property powers of attorney. There is a chapter about finding a lawyer because once you decide to make a plan, you may need someone to work with you. There is a chapter on living wills because everyone is familiar with the phrase and the Illinois legislature re-introduced them into the health care power of attorney effective January 1, 2016.

What you will not find are forms.

Thank you to all of my clients. I have learned something from each of you.

Lifetime Planning Issues

Traditional estate plans address who will receive your property (valuables) after you pass away. When I started my practice in the 1980s, wills were considered the only choice for most of the population. Trusts were considered appropriate for people with very large estates.

During the 1980s legislatures across the United States enacted the Living Will and later the Powers of Attorney to address preservation of an individual's right to decide about medical treatment, particularly end of life decisions, even if they lost the capacity to communicate the decision.

Powers of attorney are a planning device that can operate during your life if you are ill or injured and unable to make your own decisions. They are an alternative to guardianship court and are now considered a part of all estate plans.

Some people consider the powers of attorney a plan for disability.

When you look at the larger picture, decisions made about you during your lifetime are probably more important than the distribution of your property after you die.

Durable powers of attorney for health care and for property provide a management tool for you and your estate (money). They are designed to be privately handled, outside of court and not a part of public records.

The law is constantly changing. This is the third edition of this book that reflects the 2011, 2015 and 2016 changes to Illinois law.

In this 2017 edition, excerpts from the Illinois law have been added, in italics.

Chapter Organization

The chapters of this book begin with goals and definitions. The topic is broken into questions and answers and there is a review at the end of the main chapters.

I've included a chapter on how to find a lawyer to provide you with a few ideas. Pauline's Law Dictionary is at the back of the book as a reference guide.

The Property Power of Attorney

After reading this chapter you will understand:

What a property power of attorney does;

How to select an agent and successors;

How to prepare your agent to handle your finances, and

Five new words.

Dictionary

agent - the person nominated to act for the principal.

guardian of the estate - the person a court appoints to make decisions for you about your (estate) money. You can nominate an estate guardian in your power of attorney for property.

principal - the person who transfers rights to make decisions to an agent.

successor agent - the person who stands second or later in line to act for the principal.

witness - the person or persons who see you sign a document and believe you are of sound mind and memory.

What is a property power of attorney?

It's a set of written instructions transferring your rights to make financial decisions to a third person, your agent, under certain circumstances.

Unless there are disputes or complications and someone files a guardianship or elder law proceeding, the court is not involved.

What decisions can my property agent make?

Your property agent can make financial decisions including paying bills, collecting your paycheck, Social Security or retirement funds, managing your investments, buying, selling or mortgaging real estate, preparing your income tax returns, writing checks on your bank accounts and transferring accounts to other banks. Your agent can hire people to assist in the management of your estate. Professionals your agent might hire include an attorney, accountant, appraiser or realtor.

The Illinois Durable Property Power of Attorney has a list of powers transferred to your agent, they are nearly the same decisions that you can make on a day-to-day basis about your finances.

The following is a list of the powers from the Illinois statute:

(a) Real estate transactions.

(b) Financial institution transactions.

(c) Stock and bond transactions.

(d) Tangible personal property transactions.

(e) Safe deposit box transactions.

(f) Insurance and annuity transactions.

(g) Retirement plan transactions.

(h) Social Security, employment and military service benefits.

(i) Tax matters.

(j) Claims and litigation.

(k) Commodity and option transactions.

(l) Business transactions.

(m) Borrowing transactions.

(n) Estate transactions.

(o) All other property transactions.

Citation 755 ILCS 45/3-3(b).

How will my agent know what to do?

The property power of attorney agent is charged with the responsibility of paying bills, collecting monies due, protecting and managing your assets and honoring your estate plan. An attorney can assist in explaining the basics.

At the end of the statutory short form property power of attorney, there is a set of instructions for your property agent. Three of the key factors for your agent to understand are that they are prohibited from borrowing money from your estate, unless there is a specific provision for this. Second, they are prohibited from commingling their money with yours. Commingling means not putting the agent's money in the principal's account and vice versa. Third, they are directed to co-operate with the health care agent.

These instructions are a reflection of where agents made errors in the past.

Your discussion with the agent before you make the power of attorney should include information about how you manage and invest your money (estate.)

Why is it called a 'durable' power of attorney?

The term 'durable' distinguishes this type of power of attorney from other powers of attorney. The old garden-variety power of attorney was used when the boss went on vacation and needed someone to take care of the business while she was away. The power ended when the boss returned from vacation, became ill, revoked the power or died.

Here, 'durable' means that the powers work during periods of time when you are unable to make your own decisions. Often these are called periods of disability. For some individuals the agent will act temporarily, while for others, the agent will act until the principal dies.

Where do I start?

After you decide you want to make powers of attorney, your next decision is to select at least two potential agents. Your agents must be at least 18 years old when the document is signed. Ask if they are willing to serve as your agent if the need arises. Explain what is involved in managing your finances. Tell them they will be required to keep detailed records and make reports on financial actions taken on your behalf.

The second step is to prepare an asset list.

What is an asset list?

An asset list is detailed information about your real estate, bank accounts, retirement accounts, investments and other valuables. Your liabilities (debts) are a part of the list. The exact name(s) and title on each asset must be on the list, e.g. joint tenancy, sole ownership, tenancy in common, tenancy in the entirety.

If you own a home (or other real estate) include information about a mortgage, pay off insurance, homeowners insurance, your insurance agent's name and contact information, the policy numbers, dates of renewal and any other information that will help your agent step into your shoes if necessary. Include whether real estate taxes are paid directly or from an escrow account, and whether the real estate taxes are paid once a year or more as well as the month(s) they are due.

If you own a vacant lot and are required to have the grass cut, list the contact information of any person working for you and the amount they are paid.

List the location of your income tax returns and the name of your tax preparer if you use one.

If you hold assets in a trust, those assets need to be identified as such and your agent needs a copy of the trust. You need to structure the authority between your agent and trustee if they are not the same person.

If you have online accounts, keep a list with PIN (personal identification numbers) and passwords. Include your cellular phone passwords and the length of any contract for services. List your computer password if you use one. If you use a thumbprint or other high level sign in procedures, determine how your agent could open your computer if necessary.

Some individuals make up their asset list with a copy of each current statement (monthly, quarterly or year-end) on each account.

If you have contracts for services for your home, e.g. lawn or snow maintenance, security services, include a copy along with your asset list or a list of where the contracts are stored.

Are there other decisions I need to make in a property power of attorney?

There are four main parts to a property power of attorney:

selection of an agent and at least one successor;

determining when the power begins and when it ends;

a laundry list of specific powers available to your agent and,

nomination of a guardian of your estate.

Your attorney can guide you through any sections that you need help with. If you are preparing your own powers of attorney, be certain you understand the document.

Why can't my spouse take care of things if I'm ill; all of our assets are in joint tenancy.

Your spouse can manage many joint tenancy assets (i.e. joint tenancy bank accounts) if you cannot make your own decisions. However, your spouse may not be able to make withdrawals from your IRA account.

If you hold your home in joint tenancy with your spouse and one of you becomes unable to make financial decisions, you may be unable to sell, transfer or mortgage the real estate without a guardianship or pre-existing power of attorney.

Assets held in your name alone, are generally outside of the management reach of your spouse. There may be unexpected assets an agent can handle that a spouse cannot manage, for instance, inheritance. If you have stock or bank accounts in your name alone, your spouse will not be able to access those assets without a power of attorney for property or an order from the guardianship court.

Most married couples name their spouse as the first property power agent.

In some families, one spouse is the family bookkeeper and paper manager. It is important for both partners to be familiar with how the family finances are handled and where important documents are stored in case of an emergency.

If my spouse is my agent, is a successor still necessary?

Yes, a successor agent is important in case your first choice is unavailable or unable to serve.

Do I need permission to name a person as my property agent?

While you don't need a person's permission to name them as your agent, there is no obligation for a named agent to act. You need to discuss the power of attorney with your potential agent before you have the document prepared. Ask if they are willing to follow your instructions about management of your property if the need arises. You need to familiarize them with your financial system or at least let them know where you keep your important documents including your list of assets.

Do nominated agents sometimes refuse to act?

Yes, naming a person as your agent in a power of attorney does not create an obligation for them to act. That is one (of several) reasons why the discussion with a prospective agent before you nominate them in your power of attorney document is important. While some people are honored to be asked, others don't want to be involved.

Even when a person agrees to serve as agent, the time when they could serve is uncertain. They may be in the middle of their own crisis and be unable to assist you, or could have changed their mind.

Who should I choose as my agent?

A suitable agent could be a friend or family member who has enough contact with you to be able to recognize when you need help. You must be able to trust your agent. Integrity is the top quality you are seeking. Your agent should not be over anxious to take over your estate.

Can I name an agent who doesn't live nearby?

Your agent does not have to live nearby. However, if you live in Chicago, Illinois, and your agent/daughter lives in Phoenix, Arizona, how well can she manage your estate from a distance? Will your agent be able to jump on a plane in an emergency? Unfortunately that's when many agencies start.

Having more than one nominated agent is important in case your first choice is not available. If none of your agents can serve, the court may need to appoint a guardian to make your decisions.

You can talk to your attorney about nominating a third person to appoint additional agents if the need arises.

Reviewing your documents every few years or when you have a life change is another way to protect your decisions and choice of agent.

Can my agent stop acting?

Yes an agent can quit for any reason or no reason during the agency. If this happens, they should advise the next nominated agent and the principal and make a final report of all financial actions taken under the agency. All documents belonging to the principal should be returned.

The powers given to the agent include things I would never do, like options contracts. Can I cross those off the list of powers?

Yes. The agent's powers are broad because we don't know what the future holds and because each person has a different way of managing their money. Options contracts are one power many of my clients delete (cross off or draw a line through).

Some principals review the list of powers and want to restrict their agent from selling their home. It's understandable because everyone wants to remain in their home as long as possible if not forever. This can create a problem if you need care that cannot be accomplished at home or if your financial picture makes other options more practical.

What can my agent do if I restrict them from selling my home?

If your agent determines that providing the level of care you need at home isn't possible, and your power of attorney document restricts the agent from selling your real estate, a guardianship case may be needed. The guardianship court can authorize the agent to sell or mortgage your home. The court may have jurisdiction over the proceeds of the sale or mortgage. That means additional costs to manage your estate.

Some agents may decide to resign rather than to initiate a court proceeding.

When does my agent start to act?

As the power of attorney for property is written, the agent's authority begins either with a future date or event that you designate.

The preferred start of the agent's powers is when your primary care physician feels you can no longer make sound financial decisions and commits that opinion to a writing. The opinion needs to be based on an examination of the principal within 90 days of the report. This is considered an event.

Are there other choices to determine the start of the agent's powers?

This is a matter that should be discussed with your attorney. You don't want to make things overly complicated or costly. The physician determination is the strongest one.

Can I direct my agent to start taking care of things even if I am capable of managing my finances?

Yes, you can direct your agent to start acting while you are still capable of managing your estate. You can either work together, guide or oversee how your agent acts.

When you choose to hand over the reins in this fashion, you should make a writing to commemorate the terms with a witness other than the agent. You may want to consult your attorney before you put this into place.

If my agent is acting because of an illness or injury of mine and I recover, can I get my money back?

Yes. In some cases your agent will only need to act on a temporary basis. If that happens, your agent should return your paperwork along with a summary of actions taken under the power of attorney.

Your power of attorney document can include instructions to cover this contingency. If you recover from your illness or injury and your agent declines to hand over the books, you need to discuss this with your attorney and physician.

I don't think my agent should be paid for their time. Can this be restricted?

Agents and principals often disagree on this point. Some principals don't want their adult children to be paid for serving as the agent.

Each case is different. Keep in mind if your agent misses work or spends a large amount of time on your finances, they may not be able or willing to continue without compensation. Agents are also often subjected to criticism or second guessing of the management of your estate by other friends or family. They sometimes are caused to defend the agency agreement in court.

This is an item to discuss when you are in the early stages of interviewing your potential agents.

While many powers of attorney operate without problems, it's impossible to predict the volatile cases.

Are there other restrictions on my agent?

Your agent is not allowed to make gifts under your property power of attorney unless you specifically authorize them. If you want to give your agent the authority to make gifts for birthdays, holidays, graduations, or weddings, you need to carefully describe who may receive the gifts, the frequency and the amount of the gifts. Talk to your attorney about questions you have about this issue.

If you want to empower your agent to make gifts to qualify for gift tax purposes, you need to discuss this with your attorney.

If you want your agent to continue your pattern of charitable giving, your power of attorney can spell out your decisions along with the charity or charities you select.

Your property agent is also expected to preserve your estate plan. There are exceptions, you should discuss this with your attorney.

While you are able to make your own decisions, you may decide to sue or defend yourself in a lawsuit. When you participate in a lawsuit without an attorney, it is called pro se. If the lawsuit is still viable when your agent begins to act, they are prohibited from standing in your shoes. They will need to hire an attorney.

Similarly, if your agent decides to file a lawsuit on behalf of you, the principal, they will need to hire an attorney. However, if your agent is an attorney licensed to practice in the jurisdiction where the lawsuit is filed, they can represent you.

Can I appoint two people to act together as my co-agents?

No, under the Illinois property power of attorney law, co-agents (two people working together) are prohibited for statutory powers. This is a very practical provision because two people can disagree and make it more likely that you will end up in court.

You can, however, appoint agents to act in succession, or, one after the other.

If you have three or four children, you can name them in succession, as agent and successor agents. If any of them are in the middle of legal proceedings, like foreclosure, bankruptcy, divorce or other litigation, it may be best not to nominate them until the matters are completed.

If you already executed (signed) your powers of attorney naming co-agents, you should discuss this with your attorney to see if new powers would better serve you.

Isn't there a non-statutory power of attorney?

Although Illinois has provisions and requirements for a non-statutory power of attorney, it's generally used as a defense to a statutory power of attorney with flaws. The stronger plan is to use the statutory form.

Does my agent have the right to read my will?

Yes, because your agent is expected to preserve your estate plan, they must be familiar with your will or trust. Your attorney can tell you more about this issue and about apportionment issues and exceptions to the general rule.

Why is there a paragraph in the power of attorney to nominate a guardian when this document is intended to operate out of court?

Most property powers of attorney work without problems, accusations or court action. While private management is one goal of powers of attorney, if there is a problem, court is one option to settle the dispute. An attorney acting as a mediator may be able to sit down with the parties and bring them to a settlement.

There are other circumstances where the court's involvement may be necessary. There could be third party challenges to the validity of your powers of attorney. All of your agents could be unable to serve. Or if the court determines that court supervision is warranted because of bitter disputes, a guardian can be appointed.

If any of those fact patterns occur, you will need a guardian. Nominating a guardian in your power of attorney is an opportunity to state your choice.

Under the property power of attorney the court is not obligated to appoint your choice of guardian.

My attorney made a property power for me when I lived in Arizona. Can I use this in Illinois?

Powers of attorney vary from state to state, but most powers that are valid where they were executed will be honored by other states. That's the general rule. Unfortunately some financial institutions refuse to honor powers of attorney without a good reason. Keeping your powers current will provide you with more protection.

However, if you move to another state after signing powers of attorney and your agent is not acting (because you are able to manage your estate), new powers are a good idea.

Consider that after a move to another state, your nominated agents may be too far away to serve if the need arises.

My property power of attorney was executed in 1990. Is it still good?

Yes, powers of attorney do not have expiration dates on them. However, updates are a good idea, allowing you to take advantage of the additional protections the updates offer.

If your powers of attorney are more than five years old, consider if your relationship with nominated agents remains the same.

If you marry, separate or divorce, you may want to update your estate plan so that your decisions will be made by a person you trust. Illinois law has provisions for agents if you legally separate or are divorced from them. In those instances, the agents are treated as predeceased if the powers were signed before the divorce or legal separation. That leaves you with one less nominated agent. You may want to consider making new powers of attorney.

Consider, if you make a power of attorney and name your spouse as your agent and you later divorce. The persons holding copies of your property or health care power of attorney will not know the effect of the divorce unless you give them written notice.

Do updates and amendments to the power of attorney act invalidate older powers of attorney?

No, amendments and updates to the law include a grandfather clause. That means documents that were valid when they were made remain valid.

In 2011, Illinois made sweeping changes to the entire power of attorney act. In 2015 there were major changes to the statutory short form of the health care power of attorney. In 2016 more changes were made to the health care power of attorney. While the changes may not reach the target of making the powers of attorney easier to understand, they have advantages. Talk to your attorney with any questions.

Does my agent have to make reports?

Yes, your agent is required to keep records of receipts, disbursements and all significant actions taken. Ideally, your agent should make an inventory of your assets, much like your asset list, when the agency begins to function. This will confirm your asset list and note any changes since you made the list. Detailed reports of actions taken on your behalf are required. While the power of attorney law does not state a time frame for reports, making them once a year is considered standard.

Are the reports on a calendar year from January through December?

The reporting period is twelve months from when the agent starts to act. If the agent starts to act in December or even November, a one or two month report could be prepared to put the reports on a calendar basis.

Who receives these reports?

Your agent will report to you. You can designate a third party to get the reports. Considering that your ability to understand the reports will be unknown, designating a third party is a good idea. There are also social service agencies that can request a copy of the report, often called an accounting.

If there are major concerns about the way an agent is handling your money, you or a third party can file a guardianship or elder law case. The court can direct the reluctant agent to make the accounting.

After your death, your agent must make a final accounting to the executor or other personal representative of your estate.

What will happen to the reports if my agent resigns?

If your agent resigns, they are still responsible to make a final report. If they are ill or otherwise unable to do so, their agent, guardian or executor can make the report.

Can the bank require a copy of the property power before they will honor my agent's authority?

Yes, any asset holder, like a bank has the right to request a copy or to examine the power of attorney before they will honor the document.

They may request the agent to sign an acceptance of office form. This form is in the Power of Attorney Act.

If all of the agents I name are unavailable when I need help, will I have to go to guardianship court?

Under the 2011 amendments to the Power of Attorney Act in Illinois, you can appoint a person to appoint more agents for you if the need arises. Talk to your attorney about this provision. It is not in the form but can be added.

Does the bank have to see the letter from my physician initiating the start of the power of attorney for property?

No, the bank is not entitled to see the letter (medical report) from your physician. If the bank wants more than the agent's word that the agency is in operation, your agent can sign an Agent's Acceptance of Office. The form is in the Power of Attorney Act.

When is the best time for an individual to make a power of attorney?

As soon as you decide you want the protection a property power of attorney provides, you should put together a list of your assets, and pick a few potential agents. Set a time to discuss your plan with your potential agents.

Can my agent withdraw money from my payable on death (POD) accounts or my totten trust accounts?

Yes, unless restricted, your agent can withdraw money from these accounts. Keep in mind that payable on death accounts are testamentary in nature and your agent should treat the assets as part of your estate plan. This is the general rule.

The law has changed regarding POD and totten trust accounts, older powers of attorney prohibited access to a POD or totten trust account by a property power agent. This is another reason to update your powers.

I have an inter vivos trust, can my agent give direction to the trustee to pay for costs of my care and living expenses?

Generally, your agent under a property power of attorney does not have rights under your inter vivos trust unless the same person is the successor trustee.

When you have both documents, the property agent's powers are directed at completing funding of your trust.

If this is your fact pattern, you should speak to your attorney.

Review

A property power of attorney is a set of written instructions. With this document, you, the principal, transfer your financial decision making to a third person in the instance you are unable to take care of your own finances.

The person you nominate is called your agent. The second or third person in line is the first successor agent, then the second successor agent and so forth.

Your agent is not required to act simply because you name them in your document. Your agent can stop acting for any reason or no reason.

Your agent is expected to respect your estate plan with some exceptions.

They are required to keep careful records of actions taken on your behalf, and to generate annual reports.

Caution must be exercised in restricting your agent from making everyday decisions. If the authority to take a particular financial step is restricted, the agent may need court authority to override your decision. This will increase costs to the management of your estate.

Discuss the power of attorney with your prospective agents before executing the document. Talk to them about payment for their time. Explain how you want your finances handled and tell them where you store your asset list.

A power of attorney for property does not provide for distribution of your estate after your death.

The Health Care Power of Attorney

After reading this chapter you will know:

When powers of attorney for health care spring into action;

How to select your agent and successors;

How to prepare your agent to make decisions, and

One new term and four familiar ones.

Dictionary

agent - the person nominated to act for the principal.

guardian of the person - the person a court appoints to make decisions about your personal and medical care. You can nominate a guardian of the person in your power of attorney for health care.

principal - the person who transfers rights to make decisions to a third person, his or her agent.

successor agent - the person who stands second or later in line to act for the principal.

witness - the person or persons who see you sign a document and believe you are of sound mind and memory.

What is a Durable Health Care Power of Attorney?

It's a set of written instructions transferring your decision making about personal matters to a third party, your agent. It includes the power to make day to day health care (medical) decisions, and decisions about housing, clothing and food.

Your health care agent has access to your medical records and can disclose the contents to others.

Your health care agent can change your primary care doctor or other doctors who treat you.

Your health care agent is authorized to make end of life medical decisions. The agent's authority can include the right to make decisions about autopsy, disposition of remains and anatomical gifts.

Unless there are disputes or complications and someone files a guardianship or elder law case, a court is not involved.

What is an elder law case?

The elder law court division is fairly new in Cook County, Illinois. It is designed to manage allegations of financial and physical abuse under powers of attorney. It also hears other disputes under powers of attorney.

When should I prepare this document?

The powers of attorney (health care and property) are usually prepared as part of your estate plan (e.g. when you make a will and/or trust). Some people wait until they retire to make a plan and others make a plan when they buy their first home or have their first child. When you have an asset to protect, an estate plan is a good idea. If you have life insurance, a will can serve as a backup plan if the beneficial designation fails.

Many health care powers of attorney are made days prior to a hospitalization.

The power of attorney for health care can be prepared as soon as you have made the decision that you want the protection this document provides. The document must be created before you need the assistance.

The documents are not written in stone, if you make powers of attorney and change your mind later, you can amend or revoke the documents. This could, however, subject you to the jurisdiction of the guardianship court.

Please note that making only one part of an estate plan can cause confusion or something worse. Planning and a comprehensive plan will provide you with more protection.

What is the next step I need to take?

After you decide you want to make a health care power of attorney, you need to identify two or more potential agents. Your agents must be at least 18 years old at the time you are preparing the document. You need to talk to them about the agency agreement to determine whether or not they are willing to step up if the need arises. Talk to your prospective agent about your beliefs and values about medical care and how you want your day to day life to be managed. Explain your ideas about particular medical care if you have them.

If you have decisions and opinions about end of life medical care, your agent needs to understand them.

Talk about whether or not your agent expects to be paid for their time and your position in the matter. The health care power of attorney document does not contain a provision for payment to the agent. The property power of attorney has a provision for your agent to be reimbursed for reasonable expenses and to be paid reasonable compensation.

If your health care and property agents are not the same person, consider compensating both of them or neither. This can avoid some friction in the management of your personal and financial care if one agent is compensated and the other is not.

You may decide to compile a health summary that lists the physician(s) you see and any medication you use. You could include professionals like an acupuncturist, hair stylist, dentist, oculist or others you see on a regular basis.

Do I need permission from my agent(s) to name them in this document?

You don't need a potential agent's permission to name them in a power of attorney document. However, naming a person in a power of attorney does not create an obligation for them to act. Some individuals are not interested in being a agent.

Can I appoint two people to act together as my agents?

Co-agents, or two people acting together are prohibited under the statutory health care power of attorney. If you already have a health care power of attorney naming co-agents, you may want to discuss this with your attorney.

The 2011, 2015 and 2016 amendments to the Illinois Power of Attorney Act have particular requirements for the non-statutory power of attorney for health care.

If you know or suspect your health care power of attorney is non-statutory, you should consider making a statutory power.

Are you required to have a health care power of attorney when you go into a hospital or nursing home?

No, you are not required to have advance directives (another name for health care powers or living wills). However, there is a federal law requiring you to be advised about your right to make an advance health care directive, like a health care power of attorney or living will when you are admitted to an overnight medical facility, like a hospital or nursing home.

Many hospitals and nursing homes have admission packages that include preprinted forms for these documents. This is the least desirable time to make a health care power of attorney. Often, these documents are not fully understood by the principal. Documents signed at this point often contain technical errors that cause them to be vulnerable to challenge in court.

Can my agent admit me to hospitals and nursing care facilities?

Yes your agent has the right to admit and discharge you to and from hospitals, nursing homes, mental health and other residential facilities.

What other actions can my health care agent take?

Your agent can talk to your doctor, see your medical and mental health records, give permission for medical tests, medicine (prescriptions) and other procedures. Your agent can disclose your medical records to third parties. Your agent can change your primary care doctor or housing arrangements.

Your health care agent stands in your shoes and can make any decisions you could make if you were able.

Can my agent consent to surgery?

Yes your agent can consent to surgery.

Does a power of attorney need witnesses?

Yes, one qualified witness is required for a health care power of attorney.

The witness disqualifications are in the body of the document. If you prepare your own document, read this list carefully. The witness must be at least 18 years old. The health care power of attorney lists the groups and their associations of persons who are not qualified to witness your document. If your witness is not qualified, it could invalidate your document.

Following is the witness text portion of the health care power of attorney:

I am least 18 years old. (check one of the options below:

_____ *I saw the principal sign this document, or*

_____ *the principal told me that the signature or mark on the principal signature line is his or hers.*

I am not the agent or successor agent(s) named in this document. I am not related to the principal, the agent, or the successor agent(s), by blood, marriage, or adoption. I am not the principal's physician, advance practice nurse, dentist, podiatric physician, optometrist, psychologist, or a relative of one of those individuals. I am not a owner or operator, or a relative of one of those individuals, of the health care facility where the principal is a patient or resident.

Citation: 755 ILCS 45/4-10.

Additionally, if the facility where the principal resides is a corporation, directors cannot serve as witnesses to the health care power of attorney. Non-owner chaplains and social workers are acceptable witnesses along with nurses and other employees.

Do I need to have my health care power of attorney notarized?

No, health care powers of attorney do not require a notary.

I made powers of attorney in 2000 and another set in 2008. Does the 2008 set revoke the 2000 set?

This question was long debated before the 2011 amendments to the Illinois Power of Attorney Act. The short answer is no, later dated documents do not revoke earlier dated ones unless you include revocation language in the later documents.

A sample revocation clause is as follows:

"I hereby revoke all prior powers of attorney for health care signed by me."

If you have more than one set of powers of attorney, you should talk to your attorney. When new powers of attorney are made, you must give notice to any person holding a copy of the old powers. Otherwise, they are entitled to rely on the old powers.

This issue (revocation or amendment) emphasizes how important it is to keep an up to date list of who has copies of your powers of attorney.

What is notice?

Notice means to give written information to a certain group of people. Anyone who has an earlier dated copy of your powers of attorney should be advised, in writing, that you have created new powers of attorney.

Why is it called a 'durable' power of attorney?

There are different kinds of powers of attorney to accomplish different objectives.

Many other types of powers of attorney end when the principal becomes unable to make responsible decisions or dies.

The health care power of attorney is called 'durable' because it's designed to work through periods of illness or disability.

The health care power of attorney can also transfer authority to make posthumous decisions such as autopsy, disposition of remains and decisions about anatomical gifts.

When does the agent begin to act?

There are three starting points in the current health care power of attorney.

Following is the text from the Power of Attorney Act:

"I authorize my agent to (please check any one box):

_____ *Make decisions for me only when I cannot make them for myself. The physician(s) taking care of me will determine when I lack this ability.*

(If no box is checked, then the box above shall be implemented.) OR

_____ *Make decisions for me only when I cannot make them for myself. The physician(s) taking care of me will determine when I lack this ability. Starting now, for the purpose of assisting me with my health care plans and decisions, my agent shall have complete access to my medical and mental health records, the authority to share them with others as needed, and the complete ability to communicate with my personal physician(s) and other health care providers, including the ability to require an opinion of my physician as to whether I lack the ability to make decisions for myself. OR*

____ *Make decisions for me starting now and continuing after I am no longer able to make them for myself. While I am still able to make my own decisions, I can still do so if I want to.*

The first choice offers the most protection for the principal. The second choice is in favor of the agent and could cause an agent to try to step in before they are needed. The third choice will very likely result in confusion.

When does a health care power of attorney end?

There are five times a health care power of attorney can end. The first is if you regain the ability to make your own decisions. The second is at your death. The third is after autopsy and/or disposition of remains and/or anatomical gifts.

A health care power of attorney can also end if you revoke the document. Finally, a court can revoke or suspend a health care power of attorney.

The decisions are controlled by your instructions in the health care power of attorney. Care must be taken not to duplicate authority to your health care agent and your executor or trustee. However, the 2016 amendment to the Power of Attorney Act states that the health care power of attorney has priority over others who would, but for the power of attorney, have priority to make disposition of remains decisions.

Can I restrict my agent from making decisions about disposition of remains, autopsy and anatomical gifts?

Yes, you can restrict your agent. If this is your choice, be certain to set up a person with authority for these tasks, particularly the disposition of remains.

What other decisions do I need to make in this document?

There are five major decisions in a health care power of attorney.

One is naming an agent and successor agents.

Two is setting the start and end of the powers.

Three is naming your choice of guardian of your person if a court determines one is necessary.

Four is stating your preferences about anatomical gifts, autopsy and disposition of remains.

Five is whether you direct your agent on the two end of life choices. In this section, you can direct your agent to make decisions based on the quality of life or to prolong your life. Making this decision is optional.

Does the law provide guidelines for my agent in decision making?

Yes, the Illinois Health Care Power of Attorney Act directs the agent to use the "benefit burdens" analysis when making decisions about medical care. That is a balancing analysis of the good points and bad points of medical treatment. Following is the language from the Illinois Power of Attorney statute:

The subject of life-sustaining treatment is of particular importance. Life-sustaining treatments may include tube feedings or fluids through a tube, breathing machines, and CPR. In general, in making decisions concerning life-sustaining treatment, your agent is instructed to consider the relief of suffering, the quality as well as the possible extension of your life, and your previously expressed wishes. Your agent will weigh the burdens versus benefits of proposed treatment in making decisions on your behalf.

Additional statements concerning the withholding or removal of life-sustaining treatment are described below. These can serve as a guide for your agent when making decisions for you. Ask your physician or health care provider if you have questions about these statements.

SELECT ONLY ONE STATEMENT BELOW THAT BEST EXPRESSES YOUR WISHES (optional):

_____ *The quality of my life is more important than the length of my life. If I am unconscious and my attending physician believes, in accordance with reasonable medical standards, that I will not wake up or recover my ability to think, communicate with my family and friends, and experience my surroundings, I do not want treatments to prolong my life or delay my death, but I do want treatment or care to make me comfortable and to relieve me of pain.*

____ *Staying alive is more important to me, no matter how sick I am, how much I am suffering, the cost of the procedures, or how unlikely my chances for recovery are. I want my life to be prolonged to the greatest extent possible in accordance with reasonable medical standards.(755 ILCS 45/2).*

How would you summarize the agent's actions under a health care power of attorney?

Agents stand in your shoes and make personal care decisions that include decisions about medical care, food, clothing and housing on your behalf. Ideally, your agent will seek your input on decisions. However, they are not required to do so.

Why wouldn't I be able to make my own personal care and healthcare decisions?

If you are hurt in an accident, suffer from an illness like dementia or have a medical incident like a heart attack or stroke, your decision making may be compromised or impaired.

The period of disability could be temporary or last until you die. During those times of disability, your agent is authorized to make decisions for you, provided your physician agrees.

How does the physician make the decision of whether or not I have the ability to make my own decisions?

The 2016 amendments to the Illinois Power of Attorney Act direct the physician to make the decision based on the Surrogate Health Care Act (755 ILCS 40/1). Following is the text:

Decisional capacity means the ability to understand and appreciate the nature and consequences of a decision regarding medical treatment or foregoing life-sustaining treatment and the ability to reach and communicate an informed decision in the matter as determined by the attending physician.

What particular things will the doctor take into consideration?

There are many things the doctor may take into account to determine whether or not you have the ability to continue to make your own decisions. She may consider whether you have been taking your medications as prescribed and otherwise following her advice. Your doctor may look to your orientation to date, time and place. You don't have to know the time, but should be able to check your watch or a clock. You don't need to know the date, but can look for a calendar or newspaper.

If you have neglected your personal care, or developed other unusual habits, this can be taken into account. Habits that put you at risk can be an indication that your decision making is deteriorating.

You should be able to recognize the people around you and know where you live. If you are handing out $5 bills or crackers in front of the library every day, this will not help. You should be able to make your meals, direct someone to help you or otherwise arrange for meals, clothing and housing. If you wander out of the house and cannot find your way home, this is a sign that your thinking is deteriorating. For each person it's different.

I want to be consulted in decisions made by my agent, how can I set this up?

This should be part of the initial discussion with your potential agent. You could put in a direction about it in your document. The difficulty, is that we can't anticipate whether or not you will be able to have meaningful participation since your cognitive condition can change.

Under the terms of the agency, your agent has full authority to act on your behalf.

What can I do if my doctor writes a report about my decision making and I disagree with him?

First talk to your agent. Recognize the issue as the doctor declining to take consent from you for medical care decisions.

You could change your primary care physician and request an opinion from your new physician.

You could call your attorney.

In extreme cases you can revoke your health care power of attorney, but talk to your attorney before taking this step.

Is my physician bound to follow the directions from my agent?

If your physician does not agree with your agent, the doctor still needs to provide you with comfort care, and is required to assist in transferring your case to another physician. You and your agent should take an active role in switching doctors.

Who would make the best agent?

Ideally your agent should be someone who sees you regularly and will recognize if things (your decision making) change. It needs to be someone you trust because you are literally placing your life in their hands.

That said, some nominated agents could be in the middle of their own crisis when you reach the need for them to act.

Most people select their spouse as their first agent. If you are closer to friends than family, you can select a friend. If you are married and select someone other than your spouse, talk to your attorney before executing your documents.

Keep in mind that the goal of your agent is to make decisions within the preferences you state, the terms of your power of attorney and Illinois law. That's why a discussion before you name an agent in the document is so important.

I live in Evanston, Illinois, can I name my daughter, who lives in Arizona as my agent?

You can appoint an agent who lives far away, provided they will get involved if or when you need help. Will they be able to come to town to take care of you or set up a day to day care plan? Handling these matters over the phone is usually difficult.

Will they be able to address emergencies? The need for an agent to act often comes without warning and requires immediate attention.

Your choices of agent needs to be balanced with practicality and availability.

What is a successor agent?

A successor agent is the second person in line to help you. If your first named agent cannot act or stops acting, the successor is next.

Why do I need a successor agent? Can't I appoint one if the first agent can't act?

You need a successor agent in the instance your first named agent is unavailable for any reason. Your agent could be ill, dead, on vacation or in the middle of their own crisis and not be able to help you.

The successor agent is for your protection. They extend the life of the document.

If your first agent is unable to act, you may not be in condition to nominate another agent. These plans need to be made ahead of the need for them.

Can I name more than one successor agent?

Yes. You can name a first successor agent and a second successor agent, and more if necessary or you want to. If you have four children you may want to list them all, in succession. This promotes harmony even though the agents father down the list stand a low chance of serving.

If your adult child or children are in the middle of personal or legal crisis, you may decide not to nominate them or to nominate them later on the list.

What happens if all of my nominated agents cannot act?

Under the 2011 amendments to the Illinois Power of Attorney Act, you can nominate a person to appoint additional agents if all of your nominated agents are unable to serve. Talk to your attorney. This provision needs to be added to your document if that is what you want. You may want to provide that person with a list of people you would consider as potential agents. On the other hand, you may want to list four or more agents to avoid the problem of running out of agents. Making new powers every five years or when an agent becomes ineligible is another precaution to take.

Why are we talking about anatomical gifts if the power of attorney is designed to work during my lifetime?

Anatomical gifts must be made at or immediately after death.

If you have a preference or aversion to anatomical gifts for research or for transplant, you need to take the time to record your preference in the document, and tell your health care agent.

If you favor a particular anatomical gift to a particular organization or school, check it out in advance.

If the donor card you have has been in your wallet since 1972, check whether or not the school or organization is still operating. Find out how the process works. How will your remains be transported? Who should be called? Is there a cost to you? Are cremains returned after a period of time?

It's good to be prepared. This is also a good time to review your documents if you have changed your mind about anatomical gifts. Check your driver's license to see if your decision is consistent across your documents.

Can I restrict my agent's powers?

You can restrict your agent's powers but you need to be practical since the future is uncertain.

The most requested restriction in the health care power of attorney is to prohibit the agent from placing the principal in a nursing home or other residential facility.

There's no question everyone wants to live at home. If you restrict your agent from placing you in a facility, and the only place you can receive the care you need is in a residential facility, your agent will need to go to court to request to override the terms of the agreement. It will increase the cost of administration of your estate dramatically.

What happens if I recover and want to resume my own decision making?

If you recover from your illness or injury and you are able to resume making personal care decisions, the agency should end. That is part of the document you can tailor. The process would begin with a request that your doctor make a current evaluation of your decision making.

I am healthy, fairly young and good-looking, what are the chances I will need this document?

There are no statistics available on the number of powers of attorney that are used or the number that could be used.

From about 1990 to 1995, Cook County, Illinois saw a large number of cases filed in the guardianship division that were disguised altercations over powers of attorney.

Despite the cost and work involved, having the powers and not needing them is better than not having them and ending up needing a guardianship.

There are estimates that the number of people who have powers of attorney are very low, suggesting a lack of understanding of the importance of these documents.

However the statistics are consistent that we are living longer and that could mean we have to make plans for the contingency that we will need help with some or all of our financial and/or personal decisions. It could be a temporary need or one that is permanent.

Is my healthcare agent paid for their time?

Unlike the property power of attorney, the health care power of attorney form does not have a provision to pay your health care agent for their time.

You may want to consider adding it to your health care power of attorney. Talk to your lawyer.

Some agents drive you to social and/or medical appointments, to the grocery store, barber shop or beauty salon, church, to your book club or on other errands. They may drive you to the liquor store and the casino. It's fair to compensate them for their time and any out of pocket costs they advance. Consider coordinating the issue of payment with your property and health care powers to treat the agents equally.

If you authorize payment, that does not require your agent to request or accept a fee.

My family knows what I want, why do I need this document?

This document, the heath care power of attorney, records your decision and puts someone in charge. If you met with your agent and explained your thoughts and directions about day to day decisions and end of life decisions, your agent should be in a very good position to make any necessary decisions that are as close as possible to the decision you would make if able.

It is better to have one person in charge of your decisions. Some families work together in a crisis and others fall apart. Sometimes when your friends and family learn they were not nominated as your first choice under health care powers, they will encourage or pressure you to change your plans.

Does my agent need to keep records about my healthcare?

Yes, your agent should maintain records of medical appointments, diagnosis, second opinions, choices made in medical care, hiring caregivers to assist you on a daily basis and any other significant decisions made on your behalf.

This protects both the agent and the principal.

Do I need an attorney to make this document?

You are not required to hire an attorney to complete this document, but it's a really good idea. An attorney should be able to explain the concepts to you and oversee the execution of the document. The attorney can tailor the document to your needs.

Nonetheless, forms are available online and other places. Illinois residents should make certain they are using the forms from the 2016 amendments to the Illinois Power of Attorney Act. The law can be accessed at the State of Illinois website. (http://illinois.gov)

The downside to self made documents is the first time a professional will examine the document is when the principal will be in a crisis. At that point corrections may not be possible.

Is this is document complicated?

No. The amendments in 2011, 2015 and 2016 were structured not only to address harm to the principal at the hand of the agent, but to simplify matters.

Reading the Power of Attorney Act will likely answer most of your questions.

The Act has a set of questions and explanations. You may have to read the law more than once.

There are seven basic questions in the most current form of health care power of attorney for your agent to know:

1. What is most important to you in your life?

2. How important is it to you to avoid pain and suffering?

3. If you had to choose, is it more important to you to live as long as possible, or to avoid prolonged suffering or disability?

4. Would you rather be at home or in a hospital for the last days or weeks of your life?

5. Do you have religious, spiritual, or cultural beliefs that you want your agent and others to consider?

6. Do you wish to make a significant contribution to medical science through organ or whole body donation?

7. Do you have an existing advance directive, such as a living will that contains your specific wishes about health care that is only delaying your death? If you have another advance directive, be sure to discuss with your agent the directive and the treatment decisions contained within that outline your preferences. Make sure that your agent agrees to honor the wishes expressed in your advance directive.

Will a health care power of attorney keep me out of guardianship court?

While the health care power of attorney is designed to operate privately outside of court, there are no guarantees.

Disputes or allegations about the preparation of your document or about the administration of your personal care may cause a friend or relative to file a guardianship or elder law case, or to cause a social service or elder abuse agency to investigate the actions of your agent under the power of attorney.

There are a few things you can do to bolster the success of your power of attorney. One, while you are able, let your family and friends know about your decision and selection of agents and successors. Make it clear you have given much thought to making the document and tell them that you expect everyone to honor it and cooperate.

If you have old powers of attorney, be certain to advise all the people who have a copy that you have made revisions, including your doctor, previous agent and any successors. This notice should be in writing, either stating that you have revoked or amended the document. The best practice is to send a copy of the new power of attorney.

Balance keeping your powers current without too many revisions. Changing your mind too often creates an impression that you are not okay.

If you have friends or relatives who pressure you to make powers in their favor, stand your ground. If they are particularly aggressive, talk to your attorney. Some individuals will make attorney appointment for you and others will bring you new forms.

When should I make new powers of attorney?

You should make new powers if you move to another state, marry, divorce, separate, adopt, or when other life events rock your world. If your nominated agent(s) moves, dies or if they start an argument with you, you may want to make new powers. If your powers are ten years old, you should consider updating them. Updating means making new powers.

Can I combine the health care and the property power of attorney into one document?

This is a frequently asked question. While you are not restricted from combining the documents, it isn't a good idea. Combining the two documents means that you will have not only an inordinately long document, but you will expose your health care information to your financial connections, and vice versa. And, if you want to revise one documents only, you will have to send it to all of your health care and financial care contacts.

Do the documents operate independently?

The health care and property agents need to work together. Your health care agent has the authority to bind your estate for payment of your medical, housing, clothing, and food costs. However, your property agent has the right to pay your bills.

Can I appoint the same person as my health care agent and my property agent?

Yes, the same person can be your health care agent and your property agent. This can simplify things or it could cause your agent to be overwhelmed with your care.

If you have more than one adult child, you have to take a hard look at how they work together. Not being selected to be the agent, executor or trustee could cause mule like behavior.

If you have two different agents, be certain to warn them at the pre-execution discussion that disagreements will not be tolerated. Don't make the assumption that one will provide a balance to the other even if they get along with one another.

Does the health care power of attorney have anything to do with my will?

Traditionally, your spouse or executor under your will make your funeral arrangements. Today, people make prepaid funerals and health care powers of attorney which shift the decision making. It means if your will has a clause authorizing your executor to make these decisions, the overlapping authority can cause confusion or worse, two people trying to make arrangements for one body.

If you have specific decisions about disposition of remains, be certain the person you authorize to carry out those decisions has access to any necessary paperwork.

Many prepaid funeral plans are non-refundable. Don't keep them a secret.

Payment for funeral costs should be considered.

What is a mental health power of attorney?

The Illinois Mental Health Treatment Preferences Declaration Act is another kind of statutory power of attorney created to specifically cover mental health care decisions. It covers, but is not limited to medications, admission and discharge to and from psychiatric hospitals. The mental health care power of attorney has specific powers and restrictions that relate only to mental health treatment. The Illinois law is at 755 ILCS 43/1.

The 2015 and 2016 revisions to the power of attorney for health care have added the power to admit or discharge you to or from psychiatric facilities.

One major difference between the two powers (health care compared to mental health) is that to revoke a mental health power of attorney, you need to have consent from a physician. To revoke a health care power of attorney, you don't need capacity. This is another, much debated issue. Talk to your attorney if you have questions.

Review

The health care power of attorney is a written set of instructions. With it you can select a person to stand in your shoes and make personal care decisions in the event you are unable to make them for yourself. These decisions can be day to day decisions about medical care, food, clothing and housing. The decisions could include end of life medical decisions, anatomical gifts, autopsy and disposition of remains.

Your health care agent can talk to your doctor, look at your medical records, consent to treatments, medications, surgeries and consent to release of your medical records to third parties.

This document must be made ahead of the need for it. Keep a list of where you send copies of the document in case you later decide to revoke or amend the power. Remember, people who have a copy of your power of attorney who are unaware of revocations or amendments may rely on the old power of attorney.

Keeping the document current, nominating an agent who will notice when you need help, and talking to your agent about your life values and end of life decisions are vital.

If you go to the hospital, take a copy of your health care power of attorney to place in your file. Do not assume the copy you provided on an earlier hospitalization, or the copy you provided to your physician will be available.

Consider compiling a list of any physicians you prefer and medications you take. Include the frequency of your appointments. Add a copy of any prescription for glasses and the names and contact information for other professionals you prefer.

Changes to Powers of Attorney

The (capacity) requirements for the principal to change (or amend) a health care power of attorney are different from those to change a mental health power of attorney. The requirements to change a property power of attorney require capacity. In all three cases, a new power of attorney is generally preferable than a simple change, for instance, to remove an agent.

Health Care Powers of Attorney

The principal can revoke a health care power of attorney at any time. This can be done without input from your attending physician. You can revoke a health care power even if your physician feels you do not have capacity.

As of 2016, the Illinois legislature has provided for amendments to the health care power by a writing signed and dated by the principal or by communicating the intent to amend to a third person who makes a writing of the decision.

Despite this provision, making a new document is preferred since you will have a list of the witness disqualifications in the body of a the new power of attorney.

Property Powers of Attorney

The principal can revoke or amend the property power of attorney as long as he or she has capacity. While the legislature does not address the steps required, it would appear that if the agent is not acting, the principal retains capacity to amend or revoke the document. If the agent is acting, you need to talk to your attorney.

Mental Health Power of Attorney

A doctor evaluation as to whether or not you are capable of giving consent or withholding informed consent for mental health treatment is required to revoke this document. You should discuss this with your attorney before executing this power of attorney. This applies if your agent is acting.

If your agent is not acting, unless you become incapable of giving informed consent, the document expires in three years.

Can I change my power of attorney by marking the changes on the document?

No. The statutory provisions, discussed above suggests a very informal amendment process that seems ripe for attack. Talk to your attorney if you want to make changes.

When should I make changes to powers of attorney?

Generally, when you have a big life event, like marriage, divorce, separation, adoption, or if you move to a new state, you should review your powers and consider whether the changes should be reflected. If your agent dies, moves away or you lose contact with them, a new document could be in order.

If your agent is already acting, you may have to take steps to establish your capacity to make changes as discussed above.

Is there anything else I need to do when I want to make changes to a power of attorney?

Yes, when you make changes you have to notify everyone who has a copy of an earlier dated power of attorney document. This point is so important, it bears repeating. It will protect you and your decisions.

Isn't destroying the original copy of a power of attorney enough to revoke it?

No, when you destroy the original power of attorney document (by burning, tearing or otherwise obliterating the document), the copies are still out there. Therefore careful record keeping is a part of maintaining and protecting your decisions. A person with a copy of a power of attorney who is not aware that the document has been amended or revoked is entitled to rely on the document.

Review

Changes to a health care or property power of attorney are best made by making entirely new documents and complying with the execution requirements. If your named agent(s) has predeceased you, moved away, or if your agent started an argument with you, you need new documents. If you have changed your mind about anatomical gifts or disposition of remains, you need a new document. Make certain you have revocation language in your new document and make certain you give notice to everyone (including previous agents) and every doctor and institution who has a copy of your earlier power(s) that you have made changes.

Although many powers of attorney will never be used, you are wiser to have them, and keep them current even if they are never used. Life is uncertain.

If you are married and both spouses have executed powers of attorney for health care and/or property, be certain both of you know where the original documents are stored.

Maintain a list of names and dates and addresses where you send or give a copy of the powers of attorney. You will need to notify those people if you revoke or amend your powers of attorney.

Before naming a person as your agent, discuss the matter with them. Let them know your expectations and your decisions about health and financial matters. Ask if they are willing to help you if the need arises. Discuss whether they want to be paid and whether you have issues with the idea of your agent being paid. Talk to your prospective health care agent about any decisions or beliefs you have about end of life decisions and withdrawing or discontinuing medical treatment.

Discuss your financial plan with your prospective property power of attorney agent. Explain that they will need to keep records of their actions and try to keep your estate plan intact, with some exceptions.

If you are relying on a living will signed fifteen years ago, consider upgrading to the health care power of attorney.

Living Wills

A living will is a written declaration that if you have a terminal medical condition, you don't want your life prolonged by artificial means or extraordinary medical care. It's the ancestor to the power of attorney for health care.

The living will was signed into law by the Illinois State legislature to provide you with an opportunity to state your wishes about end of life medical care.

Today, we acknowledge that the living will does not go far enough to protect you. First, it is physician initiated and few doctors want to start the process. Second, no third party is in your place to make the decision. Third, it only applies to end of life decisions. Fourth, you must have a terminal condition for this law to apply.

This document is good to state your preference about extraordinary life support measures. However, when you compare the living will to the health care power of attorney, the health care power of attorney comes out miles ahead.

This analysis of the living will was included to highlight the differences in the two health care directives. It's a term many people are familiar with, but sometimes misunderstand because of the changes in the law. If you have both a living will and a health care power of attorney, the living will is suspended in favor of the health care power of attorney. Nonetheless, in the 2016 Amendments, the Illinois legislature pointed out that your health care agent should be aware of other health care directives like the living will.

While many attorneys will write a living will for you, at least an equal number do not see any benefit to it.

How to Find a Lawyer

There are many ways to find a lawyer. You can attend lectures, search the internet, read books or ask your friends or neighbors if they like their lawyers.

That said, you must keep in mind that lawyers usually practice in specific areas of law. The days of the general practitioner are fading fast.

Many lawyers will meet with you for a half-hour or hour at a reduced hourly rate or at no charge. This is an opportunity for the lawyer to determine whether they can accept your case and for you to have an opportunity to see if you can work with the attorney.

It's important you locate a lawyer who does the kind of work you require. It's important that they have experience in the area of law.

You don't want to meet with a criminal defense attorney if you want to write a will or power of attorney.

As an estate planner who does trusts, probate, elder law and guardianship, I don't need to meet with someone who is charged with a felony or who wants to file a federal lawsuit for copyright infringement.

But, if one of my client's has a need of an attorney in an area I don't practice, I will find them a few names.

If you have worked with an attorney in the past, and they don't do estate planning, you can ask them to refer you to someone who does.

Selecting the right attorney includes finding one you are comfortable with and will speak to honestly. Many people are comfortable with the first attorney they meet because they have some background information about them. Take a look if the attorney has a website describing their practice.

If you want to make powers of attorney, interview your potential agents and determine whether or not they are willing to serve if the need arises before you meet with an attorney. Talk to them about your beliefs about medical care and about end of life decisions to stop or forego medical treatment. Talk to them about your financial picture and expectations.

Powers of attorney are only part of an estate plan, they address the possibility that you will need help with personal and financial decisions during your lifetime.

While you are making powers of attorney, it's a very good time to do a complete estate plan. You will already have your asset list together and will have identified people to take care of things if you cannot.

Consider who would be a good executor if you want to write a will, then select a second person as backup. The executor carries out the terms of a will. Think about your estate as a pie, making fractional shares rather than particular dollar figures or earmarking each piece of valuable property you own. Then make a backup plan if any beneficiary dies before you do. When you decide about the distribution plan of your estate, consider bequests to charities, schools or causes.

Your attorney can estimate who may inherit your estate if you do not have an estate plan or if your plan fails. This is only an educated guess since heirs are not determined until you pass away.

Most attorney's operate with a written fee agreement. This is for your protection. It should state what is included and what is not. It should say when the fee in whole or in part of it is due. It should say whether it is a flat fee or whether it will be billed on an hourly basis. If the attorney comes to your house, ask about travel time.

Keep in mind that if the attorney prepares the documents as you direct, and you change your mind, you could likely incur additional charges.

If you have questions about the fee agreement, ask before you sign. Set a timetable to get things done, like your asset list, identification of agents, the pre-document discussion and such. Breaking it down into steps will help you.

Pick an attorney who matches your values and personality. Ask questions about the attorney's experience in the area of law you need help with.

Ask for a resume. References are difficult since attorneys are required to maintain client confidentiality.

Good attorneys come in all shapes, sizes and ages. Their offices are large, small and in between. They have offices in large metropolitan areas, the suburbs, in co-op office space and at their home.

They have huge office staff and work alone. They graduated from IIT, Harvard or universities you have never heard about. They have deluxe office machines and furnishings and things from IKEA and the local box stores.

EPILOGUE

Making a will, powers of attorney and/or a trust is difficult because it makes us think about death and of course, we worry about cost. We worry about making the right decision.

However, if you make a plan instead of hoping you won't run into illness, injury or death, you may have that peace of mind everyone talks about. Your estate plan should be reviewed about every five years or when you have a big life event as described in the preceding chapters.

I wrote this book to show you that planning isn't as difficult if it's broken down into steps and you understand what the documents can do for you.

You are not required to make a plan. If you do not have a plan for disability (like powers of attorney, or if you make only one of the two documents), the court can appoint a guardian to inventory your assets, purchase a bond, draft a budget and report to the court once a year of the financial activities.

In some instances the Surrogate Health Care Act will fill in the gaps if you do not have a health care power of attorney for health care decisions, but the physician may also request an order from the guardianship court to continue treatment.

If you don't have a will or trust, the state where you live will determine who will inherit your estate (valuables) and who has a preference to nominate an administrator. The costs are higher without a plan.

Pauline's Law Dictionary

agent - the person nominated to act for a principal.

disabled adult - a person the guardianship court has determined to be unable to make responsible personal and/or financial decisions.

durable powers of attorney - powers of attorney that survive periods of the principal's disability. A power of attorney is a written set of instructions that transfer rights to make particular decisions to a third party known as the agent.

estate - the valuables in your name alone including personal property (cars, jewelry, bank accounts) and real property (houses, empty lots, condominiums and castles).

executor - the person nominated to carry out the terms of your will.

guardian ad litem - the person appointed by the court to advise an alleged disabled person of their rights and to elicit their opinion and report back to the court.

guardian of the person - the individual appointed by the court to manage your personal care decisions.

guardian of the estate - the individual appointed by the court to manage your financial decisions.

guardianship court - the branch of the court that handles estates of disabled adults as well as minors estates.

health care power of attorney - a written set of instructions to transfer decision making rights about medical matters, day to day decisions and end of life decisions to a third person, an agent.

heir - the person or persons who will receive all or a part of your estate if you do not leave a valid will.

lawyer - the professional who prepares your will, trust and powers of attorney and explains your options and what the documents can accomplish.

living will - a written declaration that if you are terminally ill, you do not want extraordinary measures to prolong your life.

payable on death account - a bank account that is yours during your lifetime and has a designation of a third party as the owner after your death.

pet trust - a written set of instructions about the care of your pet if your pet outlives you or if you become disabled and cannot care for them.

petitioner - the person who files a lawsuit.

principal - the person who makes a power of attorney for health care, property, or another purpose.

property power of attorney - a written set of instructions transferring rights to an agent to make financial decisions in the event the principal is unable to make the decisions.

respondent - the person for whom a guardianship case is filed.

successor agent - the second, third or later person in line to act on behalf of the principal.

successor executor - the second or third person in line to carry out the administration of your will.

surrogate - a person who acts on your behalf.

testate - a person who has a will.

totten trust - a bank account you own and manage during your lifetime, with a beneficial designation of the owner after you die.

witness - a person or persons who see you sign a document like a will or power of attorney, and believe you understand what you are doing.

Author Biography

Pauline G. Dembicki is a graduate of the Illinois Institute of Technology, Kent College of Law in Chicago, Illinois. She has practiced law in Evanston, Illinois, a suburb of Chicago, for over thirty years. Her areas of practice include estate planning, probate, guardianship and trust administration as well as related contested matters.

She has served as a guardian ad litem in the County Division and Probate Division (adult guardianship and decedent's estates) of the Cook County courts since 1989. Pauline has served as an arbitrator with Cook County Mandatory Arbitration since 1990 and is chair qualified.

Pauline has lectured, published and received awards from many organizations including: The American Bar Association, Chicago Bar, Illinois State Bar, North Suburban Bar, Advocates Society, Illinois Institute for Continuing Legal Education, Chicago Volunteer Legal Services and the Women's Bar Association of Illinois.

Her lecture and publication topics include: wills, probate, adult guardianship, powers of attorney, pet trusts, the surrogate health care act, inter vivos trusts, special needs trusts, networking through bar organizations, trusts, land trusts, joint tenancies, and many articles on appellate cases.

Pauline has published over one hundred articles for attorneys and seventy five articles for the general public.

Ms. Dembicki has written three moot court plays that were produced at Anixter Center in Chicago, Illinois. She has been a participant of Law Day activities early and often.

Pauline is a volunteer for the IIT Kent College of Law, Women in Law program.

Books by Pauline G. Dembicki

Ms. Dembicki published her first book, Wills & Powers & Trusts, Oh My! in 2009; it is available in many libraries in paper format;

Pet Trusts, Yes for the Dog, was released in 2013 (paper version and eBook);

Wills, Probate and Executors, Not All Evil, was released in 2014 in eBook;

Living Trusts, The Bees Knees, was released in 2017 in eBook format.

Pauline's books are available on Amazon: http://www.amazon.com/author/Pauline

http://paulinelaw.com

Thank you.

Book Reviews

Reviews help in at least two ways: they tell potential readers about the book and provide valuable feedback to the author. What they are not are restating the premise of the book. What they are not are the dreaded book review where we struggled to show we read the book.

If you enjoyed this book, please consider writing a review on:

Amazon

http://www.amazon.com/author/Pauline

Goodreads

https://www.goodreads.com/author/dashboard

A few kind words, perhaps about the readability or absence of legal speak would be great. I can help people more with planning that crisis management.

Thank you.

Made in the USA
Monee, IL
04 November 2026

67375678R00056